INTRODUCTION

Five hundred years ago North America was an unknown land inhabited only by Red Indians and wild animals. In vast forests bears and moose, foxes and wolves roamed and the rivers, lakes and coastal waters teemed with salmon and cod. In the centre of the continent immense grassy plains, the Prairies, supported enormous bison herds that stretched for many miles. To the east and west stood rugged mountain chains such as the Rockies and the Appalachians, so imposing, yet to become such barriers in the years that followed. In the south and south-west lay what is still some of the most desolate country in the world, a wilderness of sand and rock, spectacular scenery and scorching temperatures.

The Red Indians dwelt in all these areas, their way of life influenced by their surroundings – mountains or plains, forest or desert. Each tribe had its own language and customs; some were fierce, others peace-loving. They lived by hunting, fishing and farming, travelling everywhere on foot or by canoe. Horses at that time were unknown to them and so too were guns which, when they were later introduced by Europeans, resulted in the virtual extinction of the bison and many bloody battles.

The Red Indians' settled lives were changed and their numbers drastically reduced following one very significant event. In 1492 Christopher Columbus landed at San Salvador, near the Florida coast and in so doing the 'New World' was discovered. The early exploration, settlement and development, mainly by English, French and Spanish invaders, was the start of what is now one of the greatest and most powerful nations of the 20th century.

The Spanish concentrated on the western and south-western parts of the continent. The French explored the area around the Great Lakes and along the Mississippi River, forming one of their colonies around the town of New Orleans, near the mouth of this great waterway. Many of the first English immigrants had left their country to escape religious persecution and they settled chiefly on or near the Atlantic coast. Amongst them were the Pilgrim Fathers, who chose to live at Plymouth, Massachusetts, in 1620, and the Quakers, led by William Penn, founded the State of Pennsylvania.

Many other reasons, however, prevailed for inhabiting this unknown land. Fur-bearing animals were prolific and furs were in great demand in fashion-conscious Europe. The promise of gold encouraged some, timber from the huge forests and the sale of land attracted others. Later, the commercial production of crops like sugar-cane, tobacco and indigo made many settlers rich beyond their wildest dreams.

By 1750, the original thirteen English Colonies were taken over by the British Crown under the rule of King George III. His autocratic policy, however, was largely responsible for the loss of these valuable colonies. He introduced certain laws and taxes which incurred the resentment of the settlers. One of these was the infamous tea tax. In Boston, feeling was so strong against it that citizens of the town, disguised as Red Indians, boarded the ships of the East India Company and, as a protest, threw the tea into the harbour; an event now famous in history, known as the Boston Tea Party.

This conflict between England and her colonies culminated in the American War of Independence and the establishment of the United States of America. The first shots of the war were fired at Lexington and the opening battle was fought at Bunker Hill, near Charlestown, in 1775. George Washington, later to be President, was appointed Commander-in-Chief of the ill-armed and undisciplined forces.

On July 4th 1776 Congress issued its Declaration of Independence, renouncing all allegiance to the British Crown and stating: "that these United Colonies are, and of right ought to be, free and independent states". The war, however, continued for another seven years during which time Spain and France joined in as America's allies. Towards the end only New York remained in British hands and eventually peace negotiations were opened which resulted in the recognition of American Independence through the Treaty of Paris of 1783.

Encouraged by the Mexican Government to trade and settle in Texas, the Americans gradually outnumbered the Mexicans living there. Conditions were unsatisfactory and the Texas Revolution resulted. One of the famous battles was that of the Alamo, in which many frontiersmen, including the legendary Davy Crockett, died. Later confrontations were more successful and Texas became annexed to America in 1844.

Meanwhile, many settlers were attracted to the far west, with its fine climate, good farming land and mineral deposits. Westward migration by thousands of pioneer farmers in wagon trains were a familiar sight along the California and Oregon Trails. They faced enormous hardships, shortage of food and water, attacks by Indians and lawless whites, extreme weather conditions and, eventually, the barrier posed by the Rocky Mountains. Between 1783 and 1848, however, American expansion was at its greatest. America quadrupled its size and, with the rich resources it had acquired became, by 1900, the world's largest industrial and agricultural nation.

Vast fortunes were made from coal, oil, steel, timber, railways, milling and meat packaging – to mention just a few of the boom industries of the time. Cities like Chicago, Pittsburgh, Philadelphia, Detroit and New York grew rapidly as a result, and the influx of millions of immigrants from Europe, many of them highly skilled, have made America into not only a prosperous country but also a fascinating melting-pot of races and a land of great opportunity.

"Old Glory" is the flag of the U.S.A. whose fifty stars represent the fifty states now part of the Union, and the thirteen stripes, the original number of states.

Philadelphia, signifying brotherly love, was founded in 1682 by the British Quaker, William Penn. It has many notable buildings, including Independence Hall *above and below left*, in which the Declaration of Independence was adopted in 1776, whilst *above left* the mellow wood-panelled Assembly Room in the interior can be seen.

Photographed *below* is Washington's headquarters at Valley Forge.

The Memorial commemorating the high point of the Confederacy in Gettysburg is seen *right*, the battle having been fought in 1863, and this northern victory marked the turning point in the Civil War. Franklin Field *centre right*, is a sports stadium at the University of Pennsylvania dedicated to the memory of Benjamin Franklin, the eminent statesman and scientist, and Pennsylvania's President from 1785-88, who was instrumental in the drafting of the U.S. Constitution. Night falls over the financial centre of Pittsburgh *bottom*, at the point where the Allegheny and Monongahela Rivers flow together, forming the Ohio River. The famous Liberty Bell is pictured *below*.

New York's fingers of steel and concrete thrust their way skywards in dawn's early light *above left*, in sharp contrast to the brash city street life *top right and centre right*, whilst the Empire State Building, once the world's tallest still towers majestically in the picture *above centre*.

Within the Rockefeller Centre shimmering Prometheus presides over the ice-rink *right*, and *far left* the bronze figure of Atlas lifts the world heaven-ward. St Patrick's gothic spires can be seen *centre left* and *near left* the familiar sight of the Statue of Liberty.

Docking facilities, a complexity of intertwining and convoluted roads and skyscrapers – each new structure seeming to reach nearer to the skies – epitomises the New York of the imagination which proves to be the New York of reality *overleaf*.

Amid the clamour and confusion of the city lies Central Park, seen here in many moods and differing seasons. This lovely oasis was created by Calvert Vaux and Frederick Law Olmstead in the mid 19th century and they contoured the park to the natural topography of the area. With its ice-skating rink, open-air theatres and restaurants it is a haven to visitors and residents alike.

Washington D.C., capital of the U.S.A., is beautifully situated on the banks of the Potomac River, a site chosen by the first President, George Washington. The dazzling mirrored image of the Capitol building, in the centre of this lovely city, can be seen *left*.

Standing majestically amid smooth green lawns is the White House *centre right* residence of the President. Its beauty is matched by the classical features of the Lincoln Memorial *below right* and the Supreme Court building *bottom*. Washington Monument *near right*, is one of the tallest in the world and was commenced in 1848 to mark the achievements of the formidable George Washington.

The dramatic Marine Corps Memorial at Arlington National Cemetery can be seen *far right* and *below*, Washington's underground system.

Set like an opal in a quiet oasis of lawns and soft green trees stands the Capitol *above*, in the heart of Washington D.C.

The beautiful white domed Jefferson Memorial *left*, which was built to resemble his home, Monticello, contains a 19 foot bronze statue of the 3rd President.

Abraham Lincoln, 16th President of the U.S.A., whose famous anti-slavery pronouncement led to the terrible Civil War which raged from 1861-65, was tragically slain in 1865 by John Wilkes Booth. The Lincoln Memorial *right* is a fitting tribute to a great and compassionate man whose action was to have such a profound effect on the country's whole social structure, so keenly felt in the Southern States.

Maine, in the far north-east of the U.S.A., is renowned for its spectacular rugged coastline. The lighthouses at Portland *left*, and West Quoddy *centre left* are essential on the rocky and often dangerous coastline.

Shellfishing in the area is particularly important and shown *below* are the stacked lobster pots at New Harbour, ready to be taken out to sea.

Massachusetts, like Maine, faces the Atlantic and has a similar coastline. The islands of Nantucket and Martha's Vineyard *below right centre* are two favourite tourist spots.

Boston, the capital of Massachusetts, is an important cultural centre whose many fine buildings include the regal State Capitol *right* and the sleek modern lines of the Christian Science and Prudential Centres *centre right*. The modest, but picturesque, birthplace of John F. Kennedy, 35th President, is pictured *below* at Brookline.

This unusual view *right* of the financial district shows the impressive sky-scrapers by night.

Crossed by the Green Mountains from which it derives its name, Vermont is one of America's loveliest states, particularly in Autumn, when ochre tones flood the landscape, at Orange *above* and South Strafford *right*.

The pretty houses at West Topsham *top left* nestle amongst the russet-leafed trees and *centre left* framed by a curtain of sunny yellow foliage is one of many farms to be found in Woodstock. At Green River *left* the verdant hues are reflected in the still silent waters.

Williamsburg, Virginia's original capital, has been restored to its 18th century appearance and this is reflected in the delightful scenes in Duke of Gloucester Street *right*, and Market Square *bottom left* with its quaint tavern. *Below* can be seen one of the city's most important buildings, the Capitol.

The beautiful home of Thomas Jefferson, Monticello, at Charlottesville, is shown *left*, and *centre left* is the impressive home of George Washington at Mount Vernon.

The Charles W. Morgan, a magnificent wooden whaler built in 1841 and now anchored at Mystic Seaport, Connecticut, is shown *below*.

Spectacular Niagara Falls are featured *overleaf* with white spume exploding against the pulsating rapids.

Detroit in Michigan *left*, home of the major car factories such as Ford and Cadillac, was completely destroyed by fire in 1805. Once rebuilt, the city rapidly developed to become a great industrial centre.

Situated on the southern shore of Lake Michigan is Chicago *bottom left*, which boasts the busiest airport in the world It was in Chicago that the first skyscraper was built in 1887 and the city still has many streamlined structures such as the Standard Oil Building *shown below*.

An important port and railway centre, Chicago's busy Downtown area can be seen *far right*, and *right* some of the numerous bridges which neatly cross the River.

Dazzling Chicago is seen *overleaf* with row upon row of uneven super-structures fronting the azure waters of Lake Michigan.

The Buckingham Fountain in Grant Park *right* creates a blaze of colour against the dark background of the city, and *below* can be seen the night life on Randolph Street, with the usual bright theatre signs and neon lights.

Resembling a mammoth red butterfly trapped between the overhanging buildings in the Federal Plaza is the modern sculpture shown *right*.

Bounded by the Mississippi River on the west and the great Smoky Mountains on the east, is Tennessee, whose capital, Nashville, is today renowned as the centre of country and western music.

The Country Music Hall of Fame and Museum *left* is one of the most visited buildings in the area.

Immortalised in song, the famous Chattanooga Railway *below* wends its way perilously around Lookout Mountain.

The pretty pink-roofed house *centre left* is the 'Wren's Nest', former home of Joel Chandler Harris, creator of Uncle Remus and Brer Rabbit and now maintained as a national memorial.

Georgia, founded by the British in 1733, was named after George II. The lovely Old Christ Church, St Simon's Island, can be seen *left*, with soft sunlight filtering through the trees.

Although Atlanta, the capital of Georgia, has a wealth of historic buildings, it nevertheless has many futuristic structures as these stunning night shots *right* show.

Florida, jutting into the Gulf of Mexico, is the southernmost state of the U.S.A. One of its loveliest resorts is St Petersburg *left*, where Hollywood's fairytale replica of the 'Bounty' can be seen. The sub-tropical climate of Miami *centre left*, together with its plush setting make it an ever-popular resort and *below*, at one of Florida's greatest tourist attractions, Disneyland, is the packed riverboat the Richard F. Irvine.

At the exquisite Cypress Gardens *right* the setting sun shimmers through the silhouetted trees and casts a pool of gold along the darkening water.

Delightful Palm Springs is noted for its superb golf clubs, one of which, the Poinciana, can be seen *left*. Water-skiing displays *above*, are a popular feature of the lovely Cypress Gardens. Shown in the background of a dazzling fountain display is Jacksonville *right*, an important commercial centre.
The blazing threads of gold left by the firecrackers as they explode over Disneyland's fairytale castle spires lend excitement to the night air *overleaf*.

New Orleans is undoubtedly one of America's most fascinating cities. The birthplace of jazz, which originated there in the early 19th century, the jazz clubs still flourish, as in the Maison Bourbon *right*, where the earthy, vibrant music pervades the smoky atmosphere.

The old Mississippi paddle steamers *below* still operate and are a colourful part of the New Orleans' way of life.

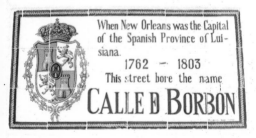

Reminders of the French and Spanish
occupations are to be found in the
historic and quaint buildings of the
French Quarter *left* and the
commemorative plaque in Bourbon
Street *above*.

The lovely Loyola University *far left*, is
just one of the city's fine buildings, and
right can be seen the modern frontage
of the Hyatt Hotel.

Texas, America's largest state, is the leading producer of petroleum, cotton and cattle. The wealthy, industrialised area with its clear-cut lines can be seen most clearly in the pictures of Houston *left and bottom left.*

Although Dallas *centre left* is famous for the Texas State Fair, which is held annually, few people can forget the tragic death of President John F. Kennedy in 1963 and in his honour the people of Dallas erected the beautiful, simplistic monument *below.*

Curving through Dealey Plaza is Elm Street shown *bottom* and *right,* the clean, graceful skyscrapers which house a wide variety of industries, including electronics, so essential to the many space flight centres in the city.

The magnificent aerial view of Houston *below right* shows the spacious city with its plentiful, open spaces.

Bathed in a golden glow, the floodlit exterior of the famous Alamo is shown *left*, where the legendary Texan defenders, including Davy Crockett and Jim Bowie, were purportedly massacred.

To Texan farmers the cotton crop *right* is particularly important and the farms are large and highly mechanized.

Guadalupe Peak, remote and rugged, *centre right* is just one example of the arid regions to be found in this vast Texan State, whilst *below* the Spanish-inspired Mission of San José in San Antonio lends a peaceful air to the surrounding scenery.

The amazing rock carvings of America's Presidents at Mount Rushmore, South Dakota can be seen *overleaf*.

Nebraska was purchased by the U.S.A. from France in 1803 and within the state are the foothills of the Rocky Mountains, fertile prairies and several important tributaries of the Missouri River.

The original Oregon Trail, a remnant of which can be seen *left* at Scott's Bluff, was 2,400 miles long and involved a journey of about four months. It was estimated that approximately 10,000 wagons a year rolled westwards to Oregon Territory after 1845. One of the old conestoga wagons that the settlers would have used is shown *below*.

The sparsely populated, mountainous
state of Montana borders onto Canada.
Modern development started with the
discovery of gold in the mid 19th
century, but today copper, lead and zinc
are more important.

The dominant Rocky Mountains
provide some of the most breathtaking
scenery; *left*, with massed trees sloping
down towards the verdant valley and
above the cattle rancher tends his herd
and the blue Rockies fade into the
distance.

The darkened silhouette of a solitary
cowboy can be seen *right* as sunset falls
over the Highwood Mountains.

Wyoming, another of the Rocky Mountain States with breathtaking scenery, contains within its confines the Yellowstone National Park, which was opened in 1872. With its magnificent falls cascading down the gorge *above left* and the precipitous canyons *left*, it surely ranks as one of the most beautiful areas in North America.

Colorado also has a number of national parks and *right* the snow capped Sunshine Peak rises above its thickly forested slopes.

Seemingly tumbling into the ravine above which it teeters is the old dilapidated mill at Crystal, near Marble *far right*.

Framed by lacy green leaves is the impressive Maroon Bells Peaks *above right* in the White River National Forest.

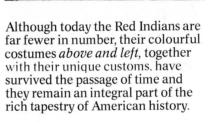

Although today the Red Indians are far fewer in number, their colourful costumes *above and left*, together with their unique customs, have survived the passage of time and they remain an integral part of the rich tapestry of American history.

New Mexico, popularly known as the 'Sunshine State', is a predominantly mountainous region where many cattle and sheep are raised. In the town of Gallup, the exciting Indian Ceremonies *above, below, left and right,* with their exacting rodeos, are a significant part of community life.

The hazy hues over Grand Canyon *left* make it a truly breathtaking sight.

Also within Arizona are the lesser but still superb canyons of Oak Creek *below* and Canyon de Chelly *centre right*.

Magnificent falls cascade over the mountains at Havasu Creek *bottom*, and *bottom right* is the old London Bridge, which was purchased by an enterprising American who carefully re-constructed the bridge at Lake Havasu where it is a major tourist attraction. The deeply etched Blue Mesa can be seen in the Petrified Forest Park *right*.

Swirling clouds in a vermilion sky sail across the black outline of Utah's Monument Valley *overleaf*.

The territory of Utah, which includes the Great Salt Lake lying in the north west, was founded by the Mormons in 1847 and is popularly known as the 'Mormon' or 'Beehive' state.

Arches National Park *left*, lies in the heart of the famous red rock country of Utah and contains more natural stone arches, windows, spires and pinnacles than anywhere else in the country.

The pinnacled grandeur of Bryce Canyon is shown *below left*.

Facing the beautiful Pacific Ocean is the state of Oregon, famed for its magnificent mountain and lake scenery; *below* can be seen the particularly lovely Crater Lake with its snow capped peaks.

The gnarled old tree *right* lends a desolate air to the quiet sandy beach at Cannon.

Watered by the great Columbia River
and dominated by the Cascade
Mountains, whose highest peak is the
ice-capped Mount Rainier *above right*,
is the Pacific state of Washington. One
of the loveliest lakes in this mountain
range is Lake Shield *left*, set like an
aquamarine between the rugged
mountains and tall green pines.

Seattle, situated between Puget Sound
and Lake Washington, is the most
important port in the state, trading
especially with the Far East and Alaska.
The dazzling night view of the city is
seen *above* with the futuristic 'Space
Needle' towering in the foreground.

The delightful coastline includes the
famous 30-mile beach at Ilwaco *right*,
lapped gently by the rolling waves.

Lying between the Rockies and the Sierra Nevada is the state of Nevada, contained almost entirely within the Great Basin.

The fast growing city of Las Vegas is the centre of a vast recreation area and well known for its casinos and nightclubs, where top entertainers perform for large sums of money before equally large audiences. The photographs *above and right* show some of the nightspots of this bright, brash city.

Downtown Reno *left* is also a popular
gambling centre and is probably best
known for the 'quickie divorce', easily
obtainable according to the state laws.

California, the Golden State, is still the land of opportunity with one of the best climates in the world.

San Fransisco, one of the loveliest of all American cities, is situated on a peninsula south of the Golden Gate, a strait crossed by the famous Golden Gate Bridge *below*. The well-loved cable cars *left* wind up and down the hilly city affording wonderful views of the city itself and the beautiful bay.

The superb Oakland Bridge can be seen by night *centre left and right*, with the glistening waters of the bay reflected in the myriad lights along the shoreline.

All the magic of the Orient can be found in Chinatown *left* which still retains its fascinating eastern culture and is particularly renowned for its many splendid restaurants.

Two more stunning aerial views *left and bottom centre* of San Francisco's famous skyline.

San Diego *below*, close to the Mexican border, has a fine natural harbour and much of its produce is exported from the Imperial Valley.

The photograph *bottom left* shows the modern Civic Centre of Los Angeles. Although an important port, it owes its fame to the glossy suburbs of Hollywood and Beverly Hills, so closely associated with the film industry.

The days of the Gold Rush gave rise to California's apt nickname of the 'Golden State' and Columbia *right* is a typical example of an old mining Township of those days.

Centre right is an original twenty mule team borax wagon at Furnace Creek Ranch in Death Valley. This valley is the lowest point in North America, lying 280ft below sea level.

Yosemite National Park is of great scenic beauty and is particularly noted for its magnificent falls such as those seen *above*.

Possibly the most famous of all is the Ribbon Fall, which at 492 miles is the second highest single cataract in the world.

With their massive trunks towering into the distant sky, the giant redwood trees *right* are a truly awe-inspiring sight.

Hawaii is the 50th state of the U.S.A. and consists of a chain of sun-drenched islands.

Waikiki Beach, *bottom left and right* is one of Honolulu's most famous and offers a white sandy beach and variety of water sports, including surfing *left,* to the lucky visitor who can also swim in one of the many beautiful hotel pools *centre left.*

The friendly Hawaiian people are always eager to entertain and share their colourful customs *below, bottom and below right.*

The chill snow-clad peak of Mount McKinley in Alaska *overleaf,* overhung by thick white clouds, is the highest in North America.